THE LONG BATTLE
Exploring Revelation 12

Vic Reasoner

2120 Culverson Ave
Evansville, IN 47714-4811

© 2025 Victor Paul Reasoner
ISBN 979-8-9937696-3-9

TABLE of CONTENTS

Introduction 4
The Attempted Coup 10
    For Discussion 12
The First Hostage Abduction 13
    For Discussion 14
Satan's Long Sentinel 15
    For Discussion 16
The Battle of Christmas 17
    For Discussion 18
The Frenzy to Thwart the Messiah's Mission 20
    For Discussion 23
The Battle of Calvary 25
    For Discussion 29
The Siege of Jerusalem 31
    For Discussion 34
Kingdom Warfare 37
    For Discussion 39
Satan's Final Defeat 42
    For Discussion 44
Bibliography 46

THE EPIC BATTLE

Introduction – THE DRAMA OF THE FINAL BOOK

The book of Revelation is a literary masterpiece. The Apostle John employs symbolic language in order to capture the imagination. Throughout the book John reminds the reader that the message is made known[1] symbolically,[2] spiritually,[3] or as a mystery.[4] However, the interpretation of this symbolism is not arbitrary. The precedent is grounded in the first sixty-five books. Thus, John is giving an overview or recapitulation of divine revelation. Eugene Peterson wrote in *Reversed Thunder* that John utilized all five senses, engaging

---

[1] In 1:1, 4:1, 17:1, 21:9-10, 22:1, 6, 8 the Greek verb δείκυμι (*deiknumi*) indicates that God teaching us by example or by showing us.

[2] In 1:1, 13:13-14, 12:1, 3; 15:1, 16:4, 19:20 the Greek word σημαίνω (*semaino*) means to give a sign. Merrill Tenny wrote that the term is "figurative, symbolic, or imaginative, and is intended to convey truth by picture rather than by definition" [*Interpreting Revelation*, 186].

[3] In 11:8 the Greek word πνευματικός (*pneumatikos*) also means figuratively.

[4] In 1:20, 10:7, 17:5, 7 the Greek word μυστήριον (*musterion*) means that which can be known only through divine revelation.

the imagination and emotions, as well as the intellect.[5]

Moses Stuart argued that John might have communicated the simple truth he wished to convey in a single chapter if he had written in prose with direct propositions, without the use of allegory and continued symbols. But John adapted the apocalyptic style of his day in order to make a deeper impression upon the mind and memory of his readers.[6]

Stuart explained that while the principle of benevolence might be conveyed by a single sentence, the parable of the Good Samaritan expresses the same truth much more dramatically. Thus, the book of Revelation reflects the oriental preference for symbolic representation of truth.[7]

The main theme of the book is *"the coming and completion of the kingdom of God or of Christ, or in other words, the final and complete triumph of Christianity over all opposition and all enemies, and the temporal and eternal glory and happiness to which this triumph leads the church."*

The book of Revelation "is filled, from beginning to end, with encouragement and admonition and consolation to all who are engaged in the great contest then going on. Victory — victory — a final and universal and eternal victory of the church over all her enemies — is echoed at every pause."[8]

The Apostle John functions as an artist, a literary genius, and a dramatic cinematographer. It is as though he switches back and forth from heaven to earth at least seven times between two great cameras. The saints cope with trials on earth by joining the worship of heaven.

---

[5]Peterson, *Reversed Thunder,* 13-17.

[6]Stuart, *Commentary*, 1:124-125.

[7]Stuart, *Commentary*, 1:200-201; 34-35; 125.

[8]Stuart, *Commentary*, 1:9-26; 155.

Unless we take frequent glimpses into glory, the imperfections of the church in this world will discourage us. However, the door is still open and we can still look into heaven (4:1). *Open* is a perfect participle, meaning that is was opened and still stands open. Those who have no interest in worship would be bored in heaven.[9]

While we await deliverance, we worship. Worship is spiritual warfare (see 2 Chr 20:15-23) and throughout this book the church overcomes through worship. John repeatedly pauses in his description of judgment to interject worship. In 4:8 and 5:9-10 the church sings. The book of Revelation contains sixteen hymns. In 4:11, 5:12-13, 7:10-12, 11:15, and 12:10-12 she lifts her voice in praise. In 11:17-18 she is on her face in worship. In 14:2-3 she sings a new song. In 15:3-4 she sings. In 16:7 she responds in praise. In 19:1-8 she shouts. Chapter 19 is the only place in the New Testament where *hallelujah* occurs four times.

The Apostle John mastered the use of repetition. The five chapters of his first letter enforce three main points: believe, love, obey. The Gospel of John is constructed around seven signs.[10] In his revelation, John uses the number *seven* fifty-four times. Richard Bauckham wrote, "There are far too many of these numerical patterns for them to be accidental."[11]

In Revelation 6-16 John describes the great tribulation in terms of seven seals, seven trumpets, and seven bowls. He covers the same event from three perspectives — based upon the three offices of Christ, as prophet, priest, and king. This

---

[9]Fletcher argued that for the unsaved, heaven "would even prove a kind of hell" [*Works*, 4:144].

[10]Guthrie, *New Testament Introduction*, 940.

[11]Bauckham, *The Climax of Prophecy*, 35.

concept was introduced in chapter 1:5, where Jesus fills all three offices. As our prophet, Christ opens the seven seals which usher in the new covenant. As our king, Christ is announced by the seven trumpets. As our priest, Christ pours out the seven bowls.

But in the middle of this epic drama, we pause for an intermission. Chapter 12 provides a broad sweep across redemption history. This perspective provides a Christian world-view. The Greek word μεγας (*megas*) is used six times in this chapter to express the significance of this vision. Our word *mega* means large, great, weighty, or decisive.

Three characters are introduced on the stage of world history:

- The sign of the woman

The church is clothed with the sun, moon, and has twelve crowns. The basis for this symbolism is found in Genesis 37. Joseph saw his father Jacob as the sun, his mother as the moon, and his brothers as stars — the twelve tribes of Israel. This was the beginning of the nation Israel.

This woman represents the covenant people of God, the church in the old and new testaments. Bruce Metzger wrote that this was a personification of the ideal community of God's people, "first in its Jewish form, in which Mary gave birth to Jesus the Messiah, and then in its Christian form, in which it was persecuted by a political power as evil as the dragon."[12] Here the symbol consolidates the corporate faithful in the person of Mary, but Mary herself is part of this corporate identity and is not to be understood as the "Queen of Heaven."

---

[12]Metzger, *Breaking the Code*, 74.

As God's covenant people the faithful Jewish remnant was expecting the birth of the Messiah.

- The son of the woman

The faithful church is expecting the Messiah. In v 5 her son is about to be brought into the world. His description is based on Psalm 2:9 and Isaiah 7:14.

- The enemy of the woman

The great red dragon is based on a composite description given in Daniel 7. There Daniel described four world empires which were under satanic authority: Babylon, Medo-Persia, Greece, and Rome. The last mutation of this beast was Rome, which had seven heads and ten horns (Dan 7:6-7). The seven heads are the first three beasts plus the four heads of the fourth beast.

The four heads symbolize divided political authority with the same devil behind the curtain pulling all the strings. Horns are symbolic of authority. The real significance is that the Lamb of God in Revelation 5:6 has seven horns and seven eyes. The horns symbolize his authority and the eyes symbolize his knowledge (see 1:4). All authority and all knowledge are consolidated in Jesus Christ. The message here to the early church is that the Lamb, not Rome, has authority. He had complete power and full knowledge. His suffering was not an indication of weakness or ignorance. This beast is *like* a lamb, but is counterfeit. Hugh Latimer, an English martyr, said that the devil is always the imitator who loves to ape God. It is the Lamb, not the dragon, who is in control.

So that we do not misinterpret this red dragon symbol, the interpretation is given in v 9. He is the ancient serpent who lied to Eve in the beginning. He is the devil. This Greek word δίαβολος (*diabolos*) means slander. The Hebrew word *Satan* (שטן) means adversary or accuser.

THE ATTEMPTED COUP

Sometime prior to Genesis 3 Satan fell from heaven. According to v 4 there was an attempted coup. A third of the stars came under the influence of Satan and were kicked out of heaven. We know from 1:20 and 9:1 that stars symbolize angels. We are never told the total number of angels which God created, but a majority did *not* fall.

Revelation 12:7-9 are out of sequence, recalling the struggle alluded to in v 4. Here John provides the heavenly counterpart to the earthly events recorded in vv 1-6.[13]

Angels were originally all created in righteousness. God could not have created them otherwise without being charged with creating evil. Apparently each angel was created individually since they do not reproduce (Mark 12:25). Therefore, the number of angels is a fixed number. Unlike the human race, angels are a company or host. The term *host* implies a military organization. The Greek word στρατία (*stratia*) means an army.

Although God created the angels as good, some of them fell. Their destiny is sealed. God did not make provision to redeem them. God did not spare the sinful angels, according to 2 Peter 2:4.

Angels which did not keep their original position of authority under God are bound until the day of judgment (Jude 6). "One thing is certain; the angels who fell must have been in a state of *probation*; capable of either standing or falling, as Adam was in paradise."[14]

Although God did not create evil, the possibility of con-

---

[13]Beale, *NIGTC*, 650.

[14]Clarke, *Commentary*, 6:951.

trary choice is essential to a state of accountability. Sin is not a foreign substance that was somehow smuggled into heaven. Sin is simply making wrong choices which amount to rebellion against God's authority. How did these holy angels fall?

- Satan fell because he rejected truth. He became the father of lies (John 8:44). The phrase "not holding to the truth," in this verse implies that he was once in truth.

- Pride brought the devil under deception and judgment (1 Tim 3:6).[15]

Pride says, I am better than the credit I get. Satan may have been an archangel along with Michael. Gabriel is often also categorized as an archangel, but Scripture never specifically says that he was an archangel. There may have been jealousy or rivalry that developed in Satan's mind.

Satan may have originally been Lucifer, but he is no longer the light-bearer — he is now the prince of darkness. Somehow pride led to deception and deception led to rebellion.

---

[15]Isaiah 14:12-15 and Ezekiel 28:12-19 are often also employed to explain this fall. Commentators debate the subject of each passage. Isaiah is describing the pride of the king of Babylon. Ezekiel depicts the pride of Tyre's king. Both employ poetic language that was consistent with the cultural and religious superstition of that day. If they do refer to Satan by extension, they really add nothing more to motives for this fall from heaven.

FOR DISCUSSION

What does this epic fall mean for us? According to 1 Corinthians 10:12 we, too, must take heed lest we fall. Do not presume that you cannot be fooled. Everything must be tested by Scripture. To borrow an illustration from aviation, we must learn to fly by instruments and not by what looks right. We must be people of the Book. Discuss how this works in your life.

Pride makes us vulnerable. The famous fable by Hans Christian Andersen tells how everyone pretends to see magical, invisible clothes on a naked emperor until a child points out the reality — that the emperor has no clothes. Romans 1:22 describes sinful humanity as claiming to be wise when we are fools. Discuss the social pressure to agree with that which is ridiculous.

On November 27, 1989 it was planned that everyone in Czechoslovakia would walk out of homes, businesses, offices, factories, and fields at noon. When noon came, every bell in every church was run for the first time in forty years. By Christmas Czech citizens were celebrating in the streets and Christian services were broadcast over state TV. A sign in front of a church in Prague read, "The Lamb Has Won." How is this a harbinger of what is to come?

THE FIRST HOSTAGE ABDUCTION

The first couple, Adam and Eve, were put in charge of creation. They were God's authorized agents and were to rule over this earth. They were created in the image of God, but they were not God. They already knew good, but they did not know evil. Satan's appeal was, if you eat of the forbidden fruit, you will be like God knowing good and evil.

Adam and Eve were tempted to become more than God intended for them to be and the result was that they became less than God intended for them. Satan used the same tactic with Adam and Eve that had led to his own fall.

Satan's real agenda was to gain control of the world. If Adam and Eve were left in charge and if they obeyed the devil, not only did they disobey God, in reality they surrendered to the devil. And so Satan became the ruler of darkness of this world and the whole world was under the darkness of his occupation.

Satan raised doubt in Eve's mind regarding God's goodness (Gen 3:1). Eve mistakenly attempted to reason with him. She added to God's law by reporting that she must not even touch the tree. Satan then boldly denied God's command, thus questioning the authority of God's Word. Satan appealed to the illusion of freedom from God. The appeal was to become autonomous from God. However, this autonomous "freedom" resulted in bondage. The result of sin was that man did come to know good *and* evil (v 22), but this acquired knowledge of evil did not lift him to a higher level. Instead, man fell and the image of God was marred.

Eve saw the forbidden fruit was good for food, pleasing to the eye, and desirable for gaining wisdom. This appeal corresponds to the lust of the flesh, the lust of the eye, and the pride of life in 1 John 2:16. Thus, she was attracted to sin as personal fulfillment. Human desires *become* sin when we choose to fulfill them contrary to God's law. Wrong desires lead to sin, and sin leads to death (Jas 1:15). Thus, the choice to sin was an abuse of the gift of freedom.

Adam and Eve did gain knowledge. They learned through experience that they would have been better off had they obeyed God and not eaten what he had forbidden. But by the time they learned that lesson, it was too late. This acquired knowledge of evil did not lift them to a higher level. Instead, they opened the door to sin and Satan — not only for themselves, but for us all.

Humanity was held hostage through the bondage of sin. While Satan did not gain *ownership* of the world, since the earth is the Lord's (Ps 24:1), he did gain *control* through us because he held us in bondage and we had been given control.

Eve was deceived by her sinful desires and messed up God's purpose. However, Mary was used in the redemption process because she surrendered. "Let it be to me according to your word" (Luke 1:38).

FOR DISCUSSION

This lust for forbidden knowledge is deceptive. We are like goldfish who demand to live outside the bowl as an expression of our freedom. This knowledge of good and evil provides knowledge we never had previously. It is like being told not to put your hand in the fire. We never knew how good it felt not to be burnt, and we never knew how badly it felt to be burned before we put our hand in the fire!

What do you wish you did not know?

SATAN'S LONG SENTINEL

The first ray of hope was given in Genesis 3:15. For the next four thousand years Satan did everything in his power to thwart the coming of the Redeemer. While Satan is not all-knowing, he was aware of God's promise — that a Savior would bruise his head. So he was not taking any chances.

He incites Cain, the first child to be born, to kill his brother Abel. Seth replaces Abel and Satan attempts to corrupt his lineage. By the tenth generation the whole world had become so corrupt that God destroyed it except for Noah's family — only eight people survived.

He questioned Job's piety and tried to get Balaam to curse Israel. Back and forth through the Old Testament this battle is waged. Abraham does not have an heir until he is a hundred years old. Two nations struggle in Rebekah's womb. All the male babies in Egypt were slaughtered except for Moses. A demon-possessed King Saul tried repeatedly to kill David because the Messiah was promised to come through David.

Satan incited David to number the people (1 Chr 21:1). At a later point the entire royal line is destroyed except for Joash who was hidden from Queen Athaliah in order to spare his life (2 Kgs 11:3). Haman attempts to destroy the entire Jewish race but Queen Esther was raised up.

Satan accused Joshua the high priest of sin (Zech 3:1). He tried to corrupt the covenant people of God through heathen practices (1 Kgs 18:28), witchcraft (2 Kgs 9:22), occultism (2 Kgs 21:6–7), and sorcery (Mic 5:12).

FOR DISCUSSION

In Joshua 2:18 Rahab was marked for rescue by a scarlet cord. During the birth of Tamar's twins, a midwife tied a scarlet thread to Zerah's hand to mark him as the firstborn, though his brother Perez (an ancestor of Jesus) was born first (Gen 38:28).

These incidents provided the basis for the symbolism of the scarlet thread of redemption. This scarlet thread can be traced across four thousand years of Old Testament history.

Exodus 25:4 instructs the Israelites to gather "blue and purple and scarlet yarns" along with fine linen to construct the tabernacle. Later, Exodus 26:1 describes making ten curtains of finely twisted linen with blue, purple, and scarlet yarns. Scarlet yarn was also used for the veil to the Most Holy Place (Exod 26:31).

Home school students might be assigned to create this scarlet thread time-line. Special emphasis could be given to those moments in history in which redemption hung by a slender thread of only one or only a few people.

THE BATTLE OF CHRISTMAS

After God pronounced a curse on Adam, on Eve, and on the serpent, he gave the first ray of hope. All three subjects represent something bigger than themselves.

- Adam was the head of the human race and through him we all inherited his curse.
- Eve was also cursed with the anguish of childbirth for all mothers (see Rev 12:2).
- The serpent represented Satan who had been banished from heaven and was now cursed on earth.

According to Revelation 12:4 Satan is standing in front of the virgin Mary, attempting to abort her delivery. While we may sing of a "silent night," in the spiritual realm it is all-out warfare.

Satan had been on high alert for four thousand years trying to thwart the promise of Genesis 3:15. God promised that the Messiah, the woman's offspring, would strike a blow to Satan's head, while he would merely strike a blow to the Messiah's heel. The heel wound encompasses all the spiritual, emotional, and physical suffering of the passion and crucifixion of Jesus. But, *in contrast*, the blow to Satan's head represents the victory of the cross — a fatal blow from which he will never recover!

Satan is not omniscient; therefore, he was taking no chances. He did everything he could to devour or consume the baby (v 4). How did Jesus get past him when he entered this world? God exploited Satan's pride.

Jesus became one of us and slipped into this world clandestinely behind enemy lines. His advent was not into royal splendor; he was born in a barn. He came under the radar and in order to do so he came humbly. The secret was in plain sight, but Satan was preoccupied elsewhere — perhaps in the major capitals of the world: Rome, Alexandra, Antioch, Carthage, or even Jerusalem. Jesus came like a parachute drop behind enemy lines. "History is crowded with many men who would be God but only one God who would become man."

While Satan dropped the ball, he kept on trying to wreak havoc. Joseph misunderstood Mary's miraculous pregnancy and this misunderstanding almost resulted in divorce (Matt 1:19-20).

Matthew 2:16 states that Herod was outsmarted by the wise men from the East. In a futile attempt to kill this future king, whom he feared would be his replacement, he slaughtered all the infants in Bethlehem two years and under and baby Jesus had to be evacuated to Egypt.

FOR DISCUSSION

Satan's method is to steal, kill, and destroy (John 10:10). While God is proactive, Satan seems to be always caught off guard. His futile attempts eventuate in collateral damage, yet he is not able to stop God.

In *Screwtape Letters*, C. S. Lewis explains that the devil cannot understand God's love. He believes there must be a hidden, selfish motive for God's actions because hell operates on the principle of power. See in particular, letter 19.

Luke 2:19 tells us that Mary pondered these things in her heart. As Mary preserved and treasured her memories, she remembered the angel's proclamation to her, as well as ostracization, embarrassment, hardship, flight, and the death of her husband.

Mary accepted God's will even though she did not

understand it. She remained committed even though things seemed to go from bad to worse. She watched in horror the persecution of her Son and stood at the foot of his cross as he was crucified. Jesus transferred her care to John who cares for her the next twenty-five years. Although most of his disciples forsook Jesus, Mary was in the upper room at Pentecost.

Today, Mary is honored and unfortunately even worshipped. While we do not pray to her, in one sense she was the first person to carry the gospel. But that honor was tempered by a life of struggle and opposition. We never win without a fight. What has that struggle looked like in your life?

THE FRENZY TO THWART THE MESSIAH'S MISSION

Satan does not rule this created world, but he and his demons rule in the realm of darkness. He is the prince of this world system (John 14:30) and the god of this age (2 Cor 4:4). The whole world system is under the control of the evil one (1 John 5:19). Satan rules over a culture of rebellion, not over God's world (Col 1:13). His rule is an ethical realm, not a physical location. The earth is the Lord's and everything in it (Ps 24:1). But the devil claimed it belonged to him by holding us hostage. As long as the human race was under the control of Satan, Satan had gained control — even if he was not the rightful owner — he was a squatter.

Jesus never acknowledged any legitimate satanic authority. Satan is called *Beliar* (2 Cor 6:15), a variant of *Belial*, which means worthless and lawless. The Hebrew name *Abaddon* and the Greek name *Apollyon* both mean destroyer (Rev 9:11). *Beelzebul* means the dung god or lord of the flies (Matt 10:25,12:24,27; Mark 3:22; Luke 11:15,18-19). These terms are used by Jesus in contempt of Satan's status and power.[16]

It is debatable whether *Lucifer*, used only in Isaiah 14:12, refers to Satan. The Hebrew word הילל (*helel*) means *to shine*. *Lucifer* means light bearer in Latin. It was also the Latin name for the planet Venus, the morning star. According to Revelation 22:16 Jesus is the bright morning star. Satan, on the other hand, is the prince of darkness. According to D. H. Wheaton, the title of *morning star* or *Lucifer* (KJV) is used to taunt the king of Babylon, who had set himself among the gods. While

---

[16]Bahnsen, "Person, Work, and Present Status of Satan," 27; McClintock & Strong, *Cyclopedia*, 1:722.

some have applied this title to Satan, "The true claimant to the title is shown in Rev. 22:16 to be the Lord Jesus Christ in his ascended glory."[17] If Lucifer became Satan, it is not legitimate to call him *Lucifer* now. Adam Clarke wrote,

> And although the context speaks explicitly concerning Nebuchadnezzar, yet this has been, I know not why, applied to the chief of the fallen angels, who is most incongruously denominated *Lucifer*, (the bringer of light!) an epithet as common to him as those of *Satan* and *Devil*. That the Holy Spirit by his prophets should call this arch-enemy of God and man the *light-bringer*, would be strange indeed. But the truth is, the text speaks nothing at all concerning *Satan* nor his *fall*, nor the *occasion* of that fall, which many divines have with great confidence deduced from this text.[18]

W. B. Pope referred to Satan, previously known as Lucifer or by some other name, that he lost in his fall.[19]

There is not a clear instance in the Old Testament where demons were cast out. There are only four direct encounters with Satan in Old Testament. Eve, Job, David (1 Chr 21:1), and Joshua, the high priest in Zechariah 3:1-5. Satan controlled the whole world through deception. Now that he himself has been deceived, the strategy must change to confrontation.

---

[17]Wheaton, "Lucifer," 713.

[18]Clarke, *Commentary*, 4:82; see also Grider, *Wesleyan-Holiness Theology*, 168.

[19]Pope, *Compendium*, 1:413.

As Jesus began his public ministry, he confronted Satan in the wilderness during forty days of intense battle. Satan promises much more than he can deliver and Jesus blocks him through the sword of the Spirit, the inspired Word of God.

In a book on Satan by E. M. Bounds he quotes a colleague, H. W. Hodge. Hodge called this incident "the battle in the wilderness."

> Christ met the three onslaughts of His wily adversary; three times His enemy retreated. The first charge we call *distrust*.[20]

Hodge called the second battle "the battle of Gethsemane."

> The second time amid legions of Devils and the curse of a world's sin, He sought His body guard; the second time they were asleep. But Jesus won.[21]

Hodge called the third battle "the battle of Calvary." We will discuss this battle in the next chapter.

Jesus encountered demonic opposition during his whole public ministry. Yet he explained that his ability to cast out demons was proof that the kingdom of God had finally come (Matt 12:28). "In the mighty works of Jesus the power of the Kingdom has broken into the world; Satan has met his match; the cosmic end-struggle has begun."[22]

Christ came to destroy the works of the devil (1 John

---

[20]Bounds, *Satan*, 95.

[21]Bounds, *Satan*, 104.

[22]Bright, *The Kingdom of God*, 218.

3:8). In order to accomplish this, first Satan was bound. However, this binding does not totally incapacitate him. Then the master of the house is robbed of his possessions. In Mark 3:27 Jesus is described as plundering Satan's house. Is it ethical for Christ to steal from the devil? Yes, everything the devil controls belongs to God.

Even the disciples of Christ cast out demons. But Satan finally infiltrated those disciples and influenced Judas to betray Jesus. Now, after many false starts, it looks like the devil has the winning combination. Judas has conspired. He has been paid off. He has agreed to betray Christ and his cause.

FOR DISCUSSION

Do we give too much credit to the devil? Do we think of him as the alternative "bad" God? This is the ancient heresy of dualism.

Satan loves to cause us fear and torment. God has not given us the spirit of fear which causes bondage (2 Tim 1:7), but Satan will gladly give us fear if we will receive it. In fact, if we give him an inch, he will become the ruler. We must bring every thought captive (2 Cor 10:5).

Satan masquerades as an angel of light (2 Cor 11:14). But is not the light-bearer. His main power is his ability to deceive.

Satan prowls around *like* a roaring lion (1 Pet 5:8). He may roar *like* a lion, but he is not a lion. Jesus Christ is the lion of the tribe of Judah. Lions do not roar when sneaking up on their prey, instead they roar in order to instill fear.

Richard Watson argued that the miraculous power of Christ and the apostolic church could not be duplicated by Satan or evil spirits. Thus, Watson did not believe that Pharaoh's magicians performed miracles.[23] "If something or someone other than God can perform miracles, then the value of miracles for attesting to Christ's divinity is negated."[24]

The evil one cannot create — he can only destroy. The knowledge of future events, especially those which depend on free or contingent causes, is not attainable by evil spirits. "Declare to us the things to come, tell us what the future holds, so we may know that you are gods" (Isa 41:23).

Evil spirits do not always know the thoughts and character of men. The knowledge of the heart is attributed exclusively to God alone.[25]

Satan is successful, not because he overpowers people externally, but because he appeals to their sinful nature internally. If the devil took a vacation, mankind would still sin because it is our nature to sin.

First John 5:18 promises that Jesus Christ keeps safe those who are born of God and the evil one cannot harm him.

The key to victorious living lies in how we think. Discuss how we bring every thought into captivity. How is this connected to living by faith?

---

[23] Watson, *Theological Institutes*, 1:156-165; 171-174.

[24] Kole and MacGregor, *Mind Games*, 79.

[25] Watson, *Theological Institutes*, 1:156-175.

THE BATTLE AT CALVARY

Jesus is on the cross. Finally, Satan thinks he is winning. Psalm 22 gives the most vivid description of the spiritual warfare taking place. The opening question, "My God, my God, why have you forsaken me?" is rhetorical. The Father did not forsake the Son. This is made clear in v 24, "He has not hidden his face from him."

However, in this psalm Christ is mocked. He is surrounded by bulls that roar at him like lions. Dogs encompass him. His strength dries up. These are descriptions of demonic attack. Just as the red dragon was not physically visible at his birth, so these beasts were not physically visible at his death.

But even during his passion, he is winning. Once again Satan played right into God's plan. It never crossed Satan's mind that Christ would humble himself. God outsmarted the devil. The Bible never speaks of a ransom paid to the devil. God never owed the devil anything and doesn't do business with him. John Stott explained,

> The cross was not a commercial bargain with the devil, let alone one which tricked and trapped him; nor an exact equivalent, a *quid pro quo* to satisfy a code of honor or technical point of law.[26]

The truth is that God did what the devil never expected. God's plan was for Jesus Christ to become one of us. That is the only plan that will ever work. And it was at Christmas that God launched his plan. At that point in time Mary became his mother and he was born into the human race. That is what we

---

[26]Stott, *The Cross of Christ*, 159.

celebrate at Christmas. "It is an absurdity to celebrate the nativity at all if you don't believe in the Incarnation."[27] Most of us put our gifts under a tree, but God put his gift on a tree!

At the cross Christ made a public spectacle of evil powers and authorities, triumphing over them (Col 2:15). Satan fell at the beginning of the first creation and falls again at the start of the new creation. According to Romans 16:20 he was crushed under the feet of a victorious church who share Christ's authority.

In anticipation of the cross, Jesus said, "Now is the time for judgment on this world; now the prince of this world will be driven out" (John 12:31, 16:11; 1 John 3:8; Heb 2:14). "I saw Satan fall like lightning from heaven" (Luke 10:18). According to Luke 10:17, the success of disciples over the demons was taken as evidence of his impending demise. Once again Satan is defeated. Verse 9 refers to him being cast out twice and his angels once. The temporal adverb *now* in v 10 refers specifically to the results of the atonement — his second defeat.

After his death, Jesus descended into hades. Satan and his demons are having a party, when there is a knock on the door. Jesus is standing there. He said, "I came for the keys." According to Revelation 1:18, Jesus Christ holds the keys to death and hell.

While the Apostles' Creed stated that Jesus *descended into hell*, Christ did not go to hell to suffer for us; but he did visit the realm of death in triumph. Martin Luther said:

> I believe that He descended into hell to overthrow and take captive the devil and all his power, guile and wickedness, for me and for all who believe in

---

[27] Hooper, *Collected Letters of C. S. Lewis*, 2:307.

Him, so that henceforth the devil cannot harm me.[28]

Jesus also ascended to heaven and the Judge issued his ruling. Satan was condemned by the cross work of Jesus (John 16:11).

Daniel 7:21-27 teaches that Satan made war on the saints and prevailed *until* judgment was rendered. God ruled in our favor! The blood of Christ settled all claims. While Satan has no claim on the church, he will try to collect anyway. We have legal standing, but it must be enforced.

Revelation 12:5 truncates the nativity and ascension of Jesus Christ. Jesus leaves his earthly mother and returns to his heavenly Father. The period of time from his birth to his ascension was the brief time from when he entered and left this world.

As the result of his atoning death, resurrection, and ascension, salvation and the power and the kingdom of our God and the authority of his Christ have been established (v 10). Now that Jesus is seated on his throne, there is no room in heaven for Satan. Christ was inaugurated as king at the time of his session. Satan has been cast down to earth and cannot enter heaven to make accusation against us (John 12:31-33).

He made accusations against Job (1:6, 2:1; see also 1 Kgs 22:21-22; 1 Chr 21:1). At the time Job complained that he had no advocate to argue his case. Satan was making such accusations in Zechariah 3:1-3. But after the atonement was made we now have an advocate (1 John 2:1) and Satan was barred from heaven (Rev 12:10). "Satan has been disbarred from his status as prosecutor in the court of divine justice."[29]

---

[28]Quoted by Oden, *The Word of Life*, 440.

[29]Johnson, *Triumph of the Lamb*, 183.

As the result of the preaching of the gospel, Athanasius wrote in the fourth century.

> Since the Savior has come among us, idolatry not only has no longer increased, but what there was is diminishing and gradually coming to an end: and not only does the wisdom of the Greeks no longer advance, but what there is is now fading away: And demons, so far from cheating any more by illusions and prophecies and magical arts, if they so much as dare to make the attempt, are put to shame by the sign of the Cross. And to sum the matter up: behold how the Savior's doctrine is everywhere increasing, while all idolatry and everything opposed to the faith of Christ is daily dwindling, and losing power, and falling. And thus beholding, worship the Savior "Who is above all" and mighty, even God the Word; and condemn those who are being worsted and done away by Him. For as, when the sun is come, darkness no longer prevails, but if any be still left anywhere it is driven away; so, now that the divine Appearing of the Word of God is come, the darkness of the idols prevails no more, and all parts of the world in every direction are illuminated by His teaching.[30]

---

[30] Athanasius, *Incarnation of the Word*, § 55; *NPNF*2 4:66. John of Damascus recorded a similar statement in the eighth century. [*On the Orthodox Faith*, 4.4; *NPNF*2 9:75.]

FOR DISCUSSION

John Milton wrote the epic poem "Paradise Lost" in 1667. A famous line in that poem reads, "Better to reign in Hell, than serve in Heaven." While that is an accurate depiction of Satan's attitude, the reality is that he does not rule in hell. He is merely a prisoner.

Wesley omitted the phrase *descended into hell* from the Sunday Service that he sent to the Methodist churches in America in 1784. He gave no reason for his editorial decision, but it is assumed that his reason was based on the confusion regarding what the phrase meant. In 1989 it reappeared in the United Methodist hymnal as "He descended to the dead."[31]

Donald Bloesch concluded, "Christ's descent into Hades after his crucifixion and death has a solid foundation in both Scripture and the early church."[32] When we look at Acts 2:25-35, Romans 10:7, Philippians 2:8-10, and 1 Peter 3:19-22, "Paul seems to say here, Christ descended from heaven not merely to earth but to Hades and from Hades He has ascended again 'far above all the heavens.'"[33]

What do you think about the report of Athanasius? In light of the power of the gospel, how do we explain the encroaching darkness? The word *occult* means to cover over or conceal. It refers to the hidden world of darkness. Occult practices surface at the end of civilizations. Os

---

[31]Oden, *John Wesley's Teachings*, 2:45-46. See also Oden, *The Word of Life*, 437-450 for his own exposition.

[32]Bloesch, "Descent into Hell," 313-314.

[33]Bruce, *Ephesians*, 83-84.

Guinness wrote that early hunters on an African safari used to build their fires high at night in order to keep the animals in the bush. But when the fires burned low in the early hours of the morning, they would see the approaching shapes of animals all around them and a ring of encircling eyes in the darkness.

> When the fire was high they were far off, but when the fire was low they approached again. As we have witnessed the erosion and breakdown of the Christian culture of the West, so we have seen the vacuum filled by an upsurge of ideas that would have been unthinkable when the fires of the Christian culture were high.[34]

---

[34]Guinness, *The Dust of Death*, 277.

THE SIEGE OF JERUSALEM

The early church asked, If Jesus won, why are we being fed to the lions? John was given the answer. In Revelation 12:6 we are told that after Jesus ascended, and is out of Satan's reach, Satan turned his guns on the church. But God protected the early church for 3½ years.

Nero became emperor in AD 54 and the first years of his rule were uneventful. Thus, he began as a lamb (v 11). Renan described him as evil, hypocritical, flippant, vain, egotistic, jealous, and intelligent, but mentally unbalanced. He liked literature, loved theatrics, perceived himself of something of an artist and musician, and ruled the world.

In 59 he caused his mother to be murdered. In 64 a terrible fire broke out in Rome and burned out of control for six days, then, after it was thought to be put out, it broke out again for two more days. Although Nero was out of town at the time, he blamed the Christians for this fire. Apparently he had been poisoned against Christians through his Jewish contacts. This began the first Roman persecution of Christians in November, 64.

Nero was a homosexual and he found sexual excitement through torture. He was regarded as a demon in human form and depicted in art as a monster. Christians were sewn in the skins of wild animals and thrown into the arena to be torn by dogs. Others were crucified. Some had their clothing dipped in oil or pitch, they were attached to a stake, and set on fire to illuminate Nero's magnificent gardens at night. Every conceivable torture was inflicted on them. Nero also dressed in the skin of a wild animal and physically assaulted young men and women who were bound, naked, in the arena. Thus, to these Christian virgins he literally became *the beast*.[35]

He will be referenced in Revelation 13, using *gematria*, the numerical equivalence of a person's name. The extant languages in the first century were Greek, Hebrew, and Latin (John 19:20). None of these languages had separate numerals, but their letters all had numeric value. Nero's name equals 666 in both Hebrew and Latin.[36] Some commentators believe that John's "code" language allowed his book to get past Roman censorship. The message would be understood by Christians, but appear harmless, and not seditious, to Roman censors.

When Nero sent his general, Titus, to lay siege to Jerusalem, the church fled (see also vv 13-16). The early church fled to Pella and not one Christian died.[37] This was in fulfillment of the directive Jesus gave in Matthew 24:16. Actually, the Olivet Discourse was an expansion of Daniel's original vision and the book of Revelation is an expansion of the Olivet Discourse. "Thus, the mother church in Jerusalem fled to the wilderness just as Israel did from Egypt."[38]

Zechariah 14 also describes the siege of Jerusalem in AD 70. As the Christians fled, they carried the gospel with them and the water of salvation flowed out of Jerusalem so that the Lord becomes the King of all the earth (v 9).

Luke 21:22 locates the "days of vengeance" during the time of Jerusalem's siege and it was judgment upon the system which did not accept the Messiah's deliverance.

---

[35]Renan, *Antichrist*, 74-89; 134-135; 153-154.

[36]Reasoner, *Revelation*, 2:80-90.

[37]Clarke, *Commentary*, 4:330. See also Tertullian, *ANF*3, "An Answer to the Jews," 160.

[38]Gentry, *The Divorce of Israel*, 2:1016.

Over a million Jews lost their lives in the siege of Jerusalem.[39] However, not one Jewish Christian died during the siege of Jerusalem. The Roman army had actually entered the temple in Jerusalem and caused desecration. Then for no apparent reason they with drew.[40] The Jews took this as a sign of weakness and pursued the retreating army. Both Josephus and Eusebius record that this gave the Christians an opportunity to escape the city. They fled to a rock fortress hidden in the hill country about sixty miles northeast of Jerusalem, called Pella.[41]

Daniel 7 taught that the kingdom of Christ was established. But even after his defeat, Satan attempted to wear out, wear down or oppress the saints (v 25), as friction wears out sandals and clothing. This Hebrew verb seems to carry the meaning of mental fatigue. Although we may be worn out emotionally, we are still overcomers legally.

---

[39]Flavius Josephus recorded that 1,337,490 Jews died in the siege of Jerusalem [*Wars of the Jews*, 9:9:3; Eusebius gives the number as 1,100,000 [*Ecclesiastical History*, 117]. Eusebius (260-340) quoted at length from Josephus and then added, "it is fitting to add to his accounts the true prediction of our Saviour in which He foretold these very events." Eusebius then cited Matthrew 24:19-21 and Luke 21:20-24 before concluding, "If any one compares the words of our Saviour with the other accounts of the historian concerning the whole war, how can one fail to wonder, and to admit that the foreknowledge and the prophecy of our Saviour were truly divine and marvelously strange" [*Ecclesiastical History*, 3:7:1-9].

[40]Josephus, *Wars of the Jews*, 2.19.

[41]Eusebius, *Ecclesiastical History*, 3:5; see also Josephus, *Wars of the Jews* 2:20. A detailed description of the Christian flight from Jerusalem was given by Renan, *Renan's Antichrist* (1899).

Satan did unleash 3½ years of persecution on the early church, but the kingdom of Christ is everlasting. In v 14 the church was given figurative wings to fly away. According to Isaiah 40:31 we are promised wings like an eagle, if we wait upon the Lord.

After the church was protected in Pella, Satan attempted to flood it with false teaching. All three references to *mouth* in the next chapter are associated with deception. But when the enemy comes in like a flood, the Spirit of the Lord will put him to flight (Isa 59:19).[42] Thus, we have the flood of iniquity and the banner of victory.

According to Revelation 12:15 God can use natural means to provide supernatural intervention. The devil is furious because he cannot stop us either.

FOR DISCUSSION

The destruction of the temple is a consequence of the events which transpired within the seventy weeks. Clarke put the latter parts of vv 26-27 *after* the completion of these seventy weeks.[43]

> The events involving the destruction of the city and the sanctuary with war and desolation are the *consequences* of the cutting off of the Messiah. They do not necessarily occur in the sev-

---

[42]Because of textual variants, some modern translations tend to obscure the meaning. Alex Motyer concluded that such alterations were unnecessary. "The words more naturally mean, 'When an adversary comes in like a stream, the Spirit of the Lord lifts a banner against him'" [*TOTC*, 18:369].

[43]Clarke, *Commentary*, 4:603.

enty weeks time-frame — they are an *addendum* to the point of the prophecy stated in verse 24.[44]

Thus, God in his mercy gave Israel one generation to repent. Wesley wrote that the old covenant vanished away when the temple was destroyed.[45] William Tong explained that the old covenant was forfeited at the death of Christ, but it did not disappear until the destruction of Jerusalem.[46] God is patient, but we should never presume on his patience. An old adage says, "The mills of God grind slowly, but they grind exceedingly fine."

Under the new covenant, we are the house of God and he dwells in our midst (1 Cor 3:16; 6:19-20). We need inward cleansing in order to be the temple of the Holy Spirit. Discuss what this shift means. We are not superstitious about buildings; instead we are to respect our bodies.

How do we wait upon the Lord (Isa 40:31)? This is not passive idleness. This Hebrew verb *wait* means to look for, to hope, to expect. This eager expectation must be based on Scriptural promises.

John Wesley recorded in his *Journal*,

> I preached at eight on that delicate device of Satan to destroy the whole religion of the heart: the telling men "not to regard *frames* or *feelings*, but to live by *naked faith*, is in plain terms, not

---

[44]Gentry, *Perilous Times*, 25; see also *He Shall Have Dominion*, 320-322.

[45]Wesley, *Notes*, 580.

[46]Tong, *Matthew Henry's Commentary*, 6:922.

to regard either love, joy, peace, or any other fruit of the Spirit; not to regard whether they *feel* them or the reverse; whether their souls be in a heavenly or hellish *frame!*"[47]

E. M. Bounds added,

Satan's method with some is to make them rely too much on frames and feelings. With others he deals the reverse and urges them to discard all frames and feelings.[48]

Discuss the tension between a religion with no emotion and a religion that is based on our frame of mind.

Discuss this statement. "Although we may be worn out emotionally, we are still overcomers legally."

---

[47]Wesley, *Journal*, 1 May 1774.

[48]Bounds, *Satan*, 108.

KINGDOM WARFARE

If Jesus won, why is Satan still fighting us? Satan fought Jesus while he was on earth, but in v 4 Christ ascended back to heaven. So Satan must once more change his strategy. In vv 13-17 he makes war on the followers of Jesus. That is us! He is our accuser (v 10).

But are we defeated until Christ returns? NO. According to v 11 we are overcomers. How do we overcome?

- Through the blood of the Lamb. That is his atoning death on the cross. His blood was the price of our redemption. Satan's accusations are groundless. The Greek verb *overcome* can refer to legal action. Theologically, that legal action is justification.

- Through the word of our testimony

The objective cross work of Christ must be applied subjectively to our lives. His blood can cleanse us from all sin. We can be delivered from the guilt, the bondage, and the nature of sin.

And we declare the victory of Christ. According to 2 Thessalonians 2:6-7 Satan is held back or restrained (κατέχω - *katecho*) through the preaching of the gospel.

But we must fight. Samuel Rutherford explained in 1637

> I find it most true, that the greatest temptation out of hell is to live without temptations. If my waters should stand, they would rot. Faith is the better of the free air, and of the sharp winter storm in its face. Grace withereth without adversity. The devil is but God's master fencer, to teach us to handle our weap-

ons."⁴⁹

We cannot learn to resist if there is no opposition. God will not allow more on us than we are able to bear (1 Cor 10:13), but resistance develops strength. As we resist Satan, we are making Satan a liar, we are bringing glory to God, we are developing strength, we learn to sympathize with those who are suffering, and we are in training for future leadership.

We have been given authority over Satan, and God uses him to provide combat training for us. Judges 3:1-2 explain that God left enemies in the land of Canaan in order to train Israel for warfare.

The heathen still rage (Ps 2:1) and the devil still roars (1 Pet 5:8), and we do not *yet* see everything subject to Christ (Heb 2:8), but no weapon forged against us will prevail (Isa 54:17). If we resist the devil, he will flee (Jas 4:7). But if we do not resist him, he will continue to squat where he has no legal standing.

How long must we resist? Until we have reclaimed everything that we lost through the fall. Jesus will never again be within reach of the devil. The church of Jesus will finish the battle. But God will help us.

As this chapter comes to a close, Satan still makes war against the saints. But we fight *in* victory, not *for* victory. Isaac Watts wrote, "Am I a Soldier of the Cross?"

> Sure I must fight if I would reign,
> increase my courage Lord.

The victory of the cross is the *decisive* victory of Christ

---

[49] Rutherford, *Letters of Samuel Rutherford*, 290. Letter #157 to John Fullerton, 14 March 1637.

over Satan. The victory of the Christian church, through the atonement of Christ and enforced through our testimony, amounts to the *progressive* victory of Christ until his return. We live between those two great events. Satan has been in check mate since the cross. This is what is meant by "already – not yet."

The history of World War 2 began with Hitler's rise to power between 1919 and 1933. By 1939 Hitler started his invasions. He conquers most of Europe until D-Day on June 6, 1944. The tide turned at D-Day and Nazi Germany went on the defensive, but the battle was not over for 453 more days - September 2, 1945.

Spiritually, D-Day was the victory of the cross. However, the battle was not over at D-Day. Yet the second world war turned at D-Day from a defensive battle to an offensive battle — which culminated at V-Day. We live between D-Day and V-Day — when Christ returns. The third and final defeat of Satan is described in Revelation 20:10.

FOR DISCUSSION

Jessie Penn-Lewis wrote *War on the Saints* in 1912 after the Welsh Revival. The revival emphasized four points:

- Confessing all known sin.
- Removing all doubtful habits or questionable things from one's life.
- Obeying the Holy Spirit instantly and completely.
- Publicly confessing the Lord Jesus Christ.

While these are sound points, the book was controversial because it asserted that demons can possess

Christians. It was abridged with those sections removed. However, it offered valid warning against emotional excesses. While Evan Roberts later disavowed the book, he personally experienced an emotional breakdown and withdrew from public ministry. Martyn Lloyd-Jones spoke of the nervous disposition of Roberts. Roberts had little theological training or experience. During the revival the Bible tended to be ignored and new visions and revelations were received. Yet no one could criticize it without sounding like he opposed the work of God.[50]

A better model of spiritual warfare was given by the Puritans.

> Christians in their successive generations are but one agency in the hands of God, and for the Puritan, with his long-term view, it concerned him little whether he was called to sow or to reap; what mattered was that the final outcome is certain. So persecution could be faced; or the appalling darkness of entirely non-Christian nations. For the men of this noble school neither promising circumstances nor immediate success were necessary to uphold their morale in the day of battle.[51]

Kingdom growth usually comes slowly. First the blade, then the ear, then the full ear of corn (Mark 4:28). This maturing process requires time and patience. Eugene Peterson described the pastor who works for long-

---

[50]Murray, *Pentecost — Today?* 154-164.

[51]Murray, *The Puritan Hope*, 235.

term subversion.[52] Discuss this long-term, inter-generational strategy. What do you believe is your role in advancing Christ's kingdom?

In 1529 Martin Luther wrote,

> And though this world with devils filled,
> Should threaten to undo us,
> We will not fear, for God hath willed
> His truth to triumph through us.
> The prince of darkness grim,
> We tremble not for him;
> His rage we can endure,
> For lo! his doom is sure;
> One little word shall fell him.

What is the basis for this confidence? What is the "one little word"?[53]

---

[52] Peterson, *The Contemplative Pastor*, 26-37.

[53] It is *Jesus*.

SATAN'S FINAL DEFEAT

We now come to the third and final binding of Satan in Revelation 20:10 after his binding in vv 1-3. The Greek verb βάλλω (*ballo*) is used in Revelation 12:4 to describe Satan's first demotion. In fact Eugene Peterson says that Satan got bounced — unceremoniously tossed out.[54]

The same verb, *ballo*, is used in Revelation 12:9, 10, and 13 to describe his second demotion. And now it is used in Revelation 20:10 of his third and final defeat.

Revelation 19:6 describes his present reign and kingdom expansion. This chapter portrays Christ riding from victory to victory across history. According to Daniel Whedon, Revelation 19 describes Christ going forth as the Word of God, "marching as a conqueror and subduing the nations to his triumphal sway, fulfilling the mission of the second Psalm."[55]

> As the gospel progresses throughout the world it will win, and win, and win, until all kingdoms become the kingdoms of our Lord, and of His Christ; and He will reign forever and ever. We must not concede to the enemy even one square inch of ground in heaven or on earth. Christ and His army are riding forth, conquering and to conquer, and we through Him will inherit all things.[56]

Ray Summers wrote,

---

[54]Peterson, *Reversed Thunder*, 120.

[55]Whedon, "Quarterly Book-Table," 616.

[56]Chilton, *Paradise Restored*, 192.

Christ is pictured as coming down from heaven, but this does not picture the second coming of Christ which we find discussed elsewhere in the New Testament. This scene graphically represents his coming to the aid of persecuted Christians with heavenly assistance in their spiritual struggles.[57]

As a result of the atoning death of Christ and the drawing of the Holy Spirit there will be people in heaven from every *nation, language,* and *ethnic group*, according to Revelation 5:9, 7:9, 10:11, 11:9, 13:7, 14:6, 17:15. If everyone in heaven was saved on earth, the church must first evangelize the whole world by penetrating every political division, every linguistic barrier, and every cultural identity.[58] This phrase is so significant that it occurs in some form seven times in Daniel and seven times in Revelation.

The earth will know a time of peace as the rule of Christ extends from sea to sea (Zech 9:10). Nations will be governed by the law of God, and the knowledge of the glory of the Lord will fill the earth (Hab 2:14). After the world has known peace and prosperity for an indefinite period of time, Satan will be loosed for a short time — in contrast to a "thousand" years — to test the nations.

Just as sin entered a perfect environment tempting Adam and Eve, it is consistent with God's purposes that those who have seen the golden age also are tested. God's children will always be tested.

And so Paul explained to the church in Thessalonica that

---

[57] Summers, *Worthy is the Lamb*, 199.

[58] I understand a fourth term, *ethnos*, to be the most general term which includes nation, language, and ethnic or cultural group. See Reasoner, *Revelation*, 1:285-287.

Christ had not already returned. He will not return until after there comes a falling away (2 Thess 2:1-12). But this final apostasy cannot happen until the world has first turned to Christ. Then there will be a short-lived rebellion, in contrast to a thousand-year age of blessing. Satan will try one final time to overthrow the kingdom of God, but Christ will return like fire coming down from heaven. Satan will be cast into the lake of fire, the dead will be raised, and all the world judged by Christ.

The second advent occurs *after* the millennium of Revelation 20:1-6. Christ comes in vv 7-14 to raise the dead and judge the world.

Paul tells us that Satan will be overthrown with the breath of his mouth and the splendor of his presence. John, in Revelation 20:9, describes the coming of Christ like fire which falls from heaven and consumes them. All who have rejected Christ will be cast into hell, and all who have overcome will enter heaven.

FOR DISCUSSION

If Christ can destroy Satan merely by his overwhelming presence, why doesn't he hurry up and do it? Apparently God's ultimate goal is not to destroy Satan. His master plan is to raise up a covenant people who trust him unconditionally and serve him faithfully. God will dispose of the devil once he no longer serves any useful purpose. God is more interested in the development of his children than in the success of their work. In the meantime Satan functions as a "useful idiot," or to use Rutherford's quaint phrase, as a "master fencer."[59]

---

[59]see p. 37

The last book in the *Chronicles of Narnia* is *The Last Battle*. It is about what happens when Aslan, the Great Emperor from Over the Sea, returns to Narnia to destroy evil and reward good. "Further up and further in" is what happens after destruction and all the heroes and heroines of all Narnian history reach Aslan's How (our heaven). It is surrounded by a high wall, and there is only one way in. But once the latest arrivals enter the gate, they find this true Narnia to be bigger on the inside than it is on the outside. And no matter how high we climb, no matter how far into them we look and follow, we will never exhaust any of them.[60]

Discuss how this phrase "further up and further in" expresses God's ultimate plan for us.

---

[60]Sillings, "Further Up and Further In," 7-9.

BIBLIOGRAPHY

Athanasius. *Selected Works and Letters: A Select Library of Nicene and Post-Nicene Fathers of the Christian Church.* Second Series. Vol. 4. Philip Schaff and Henry Wace, eds. 1891. Reprint, Grand Rapids: Eerdmans, 1978. [*NPNF*]

Bahnsen, Greg L. "The Person, Work, and Present Status of Satan." *The Journal of Christian Reconstruction.* 1:2 (Winter 1974) 11-43.

Bauckham, Richard. *The Climax of Prophecy.* Edinburgh: T & T Clark, 1993.

Beale, Gregory K. *The New International Greek Testament Commentary: The Book of Revelation.* Grand Rapids: Eerdmans, 1999.

Bloesch, Donald G. "Descent into Hell (Hades)." *Evangelical Dictionary of Theology.* Walter A. Elwell, ed. Grand Rapids: Baker, 1984.

Bounds, E. M. *Satan: His Personality, Power and Overthrow.* 1922. Reprint, Grand Rapids: Baker, 1972.

Bright, John. *The Kingdom of God.* Nashville: Abingdon, 1953.

Bruce, F. F. *The Epistle to the Ephesians.* London: Pickering & Inglis, 1961.

Chilton, David. *Paradise Restored.* Tyler, TX: Reconstruction, 1985.

Clarke, Adam. *The Holy Bible, Containing the Old and*

New Testaments: The Text Carefully Printed from the Most Correct Copies of the Present Authorized Translations, Including the Marginal reading and Parallel Tests; with a Commentary and Critical Notes, Designed as a help to a Better Understanding of the Sacred Writings. 6 vols. 1811-1825. Reprint, Nashville: Abingdon, 1950.

Eusebius Pamphilus. *The Ecclesiastical History.* Kirsopp Lake, transl. London: Harvard University Press, 1926.

Fletcher, John. *The Works of the Reverend John Fletcher.* 4 vols. 1833. Reprint, Salem, OH: Schmul, 1974.

Gentry, Kenneth L. Jr. *Perilous Times.* Texarkana, AR: Co venant Media Press, 1999.

_____. *He Shall Have Dominion.* Tyler, TX: Institute for Christian Economics, 1992.

_____. *The Divorce of Israel: A Redemptive-Historical Interpretation of Revelation.* 2 vols. Vallecito, CA: Chalcedon Foundation, 2024.

Grider J. Kenneth. *A Wesleyan-Holiness Theology.* Kansas City: Beacon Hill, 1994.

Guinness, Os. *The Dust of Death.* Downers Grove, IL: InterVarsity, 1973.

Guthrie, Donald. *New Testament Introduction.* 3rd ed. Downers Grove, IL: InterVarsity, 1970.

Hooper, Walter, ed. *The Collected Letters of C. S. Lewis.* 3 vols. New York: Harper-Collins, 2004-2007.

Johnson, Dennis E. *Triumph of the Lamb: A Commentary on Revelation.* Phillipsburg, NJ: P&R, 2001.

Josephus, Flavius. *Complete Works of Josephus.* William Whiston, ed. Grand Rapids: Kregel, 1960.

Kole, André and Jerry MacGregor. *Mind Games: Exposing Today's Psychics, Frauds, and False Spiritual Phenomena*, Eugene, OR: Harvest House, 1998.

Lewis. C. S. *The Screwtape Letters*. 1942. Reprint, New York: HarperCollins, 2001.

_____. *The Last Battle*. 1956. Reprint, New York: Collier, 1970.

Metzger, Bruce M. *Breaking the Code: Understanding the Book of Revelation*. Nashville: Abingdon, 1993.

McClintock, John and James Strong. *Cyclopedia of Biblical, Theological, and Ecclesiastical Literature*. 12 vols. 1867-1887. Reprint, Grand Rapids: Baker, 1981.

Motyer, Alec J. *Tyndale Old Testament Commentaries: Isaiah*. Vol. 18. Downers Grove, IL: InterVarsity, 1999.

Murray, Iain H. *Pentecost — Today?* Edinburgh: Banner of Truth Trust, 1998.

_____. *The Puritan Hope: A Study in Revival and the Interpretation of Prophecy*. Edinburgh: Banner of Truth Trust, 1971.

Oden, Thomas C. *The Word of Life: Systematic Theology: Volume Two*. San Francisco: Harper & Row, 1989.

_____. *John Wesley's Teachings*. 4 vols. Grand Rapids: Zondervan, 2012-2014.

Penn-Lewis, Jessie. *War on the Saints*. 1912. Abridged ed. Ft. Washington, PA: Christian Literature Crusade, 1977.

Peterson, Eugene H. *Reversed Thunder*. San Francisco: HarperCollins, 1988.

_____. *The Contemplative Pastor*. 1989. Reprint, Grand Rapids: Eerdmans, 1993.

Pope, William Burt. *A Compendium of Christian Theology*. 3 vols. London: Wesleyan Conference Office, 1880.

Reasoner, Vic. *A Fundamental Wesleyan Commentary on Revelation 1-9*. 2nd ed. Evansville, IN: Fundamental Wesleyan, 2023.

Renan, Joseph Ernest. *Renan's Antichrist*. London: Walter Scott, 1899.

Rutherford, Samuel. *Letters of Samuel Rutherford*. London: Oliphant Anderson & Ferrier, 1891.

Sillings, William H. "Further Up and Further In." *The Arminian Magazine* 43:1 (Spring 2025) 7-9.

Summers, Ray. *Worthy is the Lamb: An Interpretation of Revelation*. Nashville: Broadman, 1951.

Stott, John R. W. *The Cross of Christ*. Downers Grove, IL: InterVarsity, 1986.

Stuart, Moses. *A Commentary on the Apocalypse*. 2 vols. 1845. Reprint, Eugene, OR: Wipf and Stock, 2001.

Tenney, Merrill C. *Interpreting Revelation*. Grand Rapids: Eerdmans, 1957.

Tertullian, *An Answer to the Jews*. *The Ante-Nicene Fathers*. Vol. 3. Alexander Roberts and James Donaldson, eds. 1885. Reprint, Grand Rapids: Eerdmans, 1978. [*ANF*]

Tong, William. *Matthew Henry's Commentary on the Whole Bible*. 6 vols. 1662-1714. Reprinted, McLean, VA: MacDonald, n. d.

Watson, Richard. *Theological Institutes*. 2 vols. 1823-1829. Reprint, New York: Hunt & Eaton, 1889.

Wesley, John, *Explanatory Notes Upon the Old Testament*. 3 vols. 1765. Reprint, Salem, OH: Schmul. 1975.

Wheaton, D. H. "Lucifer." *New Bible Dictionary*. J. D. Douglas, ed. Wheaton, IL: Tyndale House, 1982.

Whedon, Daniel D. "Quarterly Book-Table." *Methodist Quarterly Review* 50 (Oct 1868) 615-617.

www.ingramcontent.com/pod-product-compliance
Lightning Source LLC
Chambersburg PA
CBHW070040070426
42449CB00012BA/3120